GW00586036

# The Camborne-Redruth Electric Tramway System

by

## Paddy Bradley

First published in August 2005 by Randigall Books.
Copyright Randigall Books
A CIP catalogue record for this book is available from the British Library.

ISBN 0-9550755-0-5

Typeset in Comic Sans 9 / 10points by Randigall Books.
Randigall Books
St. Day
Cornwall - TR16 5LH.

# Preface

During the last thirty years or so of collecting postcards and photographs of Redruth and the district, one section has aroused my interest more than most. That section is the one that relates to the Camborne - Redruth Electric Tramway System.

I was very lucky in some ways in that I met and became very friendly with Fisher Barham, of Falmouth, who was also an avid collector. It was Fisher Barham who, in 1972, produced the book *Cornwall's Electric Tramcars*. When he decided to give up collecting he gave me the opportunity to purchase his collection of tramway postcards and pictures; an opportunity I readily accepted.

It was the combination of these photographs combined with my own collection that made this book possible.

I would therefore like to dedicate this book to the memory of the late Fisher Barham and all those people who worked on the tramway system. To my wife Margaret, for without her patience and understanding none of this would have been possible.

# Acknowledgements
Terry Knight and all his staff at the Cornwall Centre, Redruth,
Tricia and David Rowe for taking the time to read through the text.

# The Camborne - Redruth Tramway System

**A** few years ago, November 2002 to be exact, was the centenary of a unique form of transport for this part of the country; the Camborne - Redruth Tramway System. To celebrate the occasion several events were staged locally and revived an interest in this fascinating means of transport.

However, let us go back to the beginning when a company called The Urban Electric Supply Co. Ltd. was formed to "supply and set up" generating stations throughout the country. At about that time the same company applied for powers to set up tramway systems. Only two were put into operation; one in Glossop, Derbyshire, the other between Camborne and Redruth.

At the outset there were several objections, mainly from the Great Western Railway and local councils. Those objections were that the G.W.R. provided adequate public transport, whilst the councils said that the roads were too narrow for such large vehicles.

Eventually, in 1900, permission was given for the project to go ahead. The envisaged route between the two towns was just over three miles from terminus to terminus. Contracts were placed with Edmundson's Electric Corporation to provide the bulk of the system; to British Thompson Houston for the control gear; whilst the trams were to be provided by G.P. Milne, of Birkenhead.

April 1902 saw the start of laying the track, Mrs. Hanning, wife of the first general manager, cut the first piece of earth at the site of the terminus at West End, Redruth. Good progress was made on the construction of the track so that by June almost half was laid. By August, the Camborne terminus at Trelowarren Street junction of Commercial Square was reached. However, completion of the whole route was not achieved until October 1902.

To get some idea of the route examine the diagram shown on page 11. Basically it followed along the A30 starting at West End, Redruth, and passed through Barncoose, Rounding Walls, Illogan Highway, Pool, Trevenson, Tuckingmill, Roskear and finally Trelowarren Street, Camborne.

Between the two towns was an area steeped in industrial history; mines whose names were known all over the world, East Pool and Agar, South Crofty. There were also famous engineering works such as Holman Bros. mining engineers, Climax Rock Drill Co. and the Bickford Smith Dynamite and Fuse factory.

Again, looking at the diagram of the route, it shows that there were eight passing loops and three locations where the G.W.R. had mineral branch lines crossing. It also shows where their own mineral branch lines joined the main route and travelled over it to the ore crushing plant at Tolvaddon. Also shown is the tram depot and generating station at the top of East Hill, Tuckingmill.

Having given some idea of the actual track layout, what of the trams themselves?

G.F. Milne, the tram constructors, delivered them partially completed to the G.W.R. station at Carn Brea; ironic considering the opposition that the G.W.R. had put up to the construction of the route. On delivery at Carn Brea the company used workers from the mines to off-load them as they thought their expertise in handling heavy machinery would be of great benefit for the task.

Once at the depot, building of the trams was completed. Altogether there were eight passenger trams - six double deck and two single deck, plus two mineral trams. Having completed construction, test runs between the depot and Pool were undertaken using local workmen and children as "ballast"; a treat for all those lucky enough to enjoy a free ride.

Before the official opening it was possible to travel over the whole route, so on the 1st October, 1902, with the general manager, Mr. Hanning, at the controls, Tram No.1 was

6

driven to Camborne where it picked up members of the council. They were then driven to Redruth to pick up Redruth's councillors and then taken back to the depot and given a conducted tour of the works. Wives of the officials were picked up by single deck Tram No. 5 and also taken to the depot where they were later served tea.

Finally, after another month had passed, the eagerly awaited day arrived. The Board of Trade inspection was carried out under the eagle eye of a Major Pringle; apart from a few minor recommendations the route was passed fit for service.

Friday 7th November, 1902, was the day selected for the official opening of the Camborne - Redruth Electric Tramway system, combined with the provision of electricity to the people of Camborne and Redruth. Six trams - three to Camborne, three to Redruth - were used to pick up local dignitaries and their wives (some two hundred all told) and took them to the depot where they were entertained to lunch. After lunch numerous speeches were made extolling the virtues of electricity and the new tramway system. Mrs. Wigham, wife of an Edmundson's director, was then formally asked to open the system by turning on the lighting current for the first time.

What of the trams themselves? The double deck trams were twenty-eight feet long, weighed eleven tons and carried forty-eight passengers - twenty-two on the lower level and twenty-six on the upper. The single deck trams, based on the American style, could take thirty-four passengers. Livery for all the passenger trams was the same; dark green and cream with the Camborne - Redruth Tramway logo across the central panel. The mineral trams are covered in a later section (see page 65).

During and after construction of the route, various incidents took place which warrant a mention.

Firstly the "strike"; the one and only stoppage during the construction of the route. Labourers employed to lay the track decided that four (old) pence an hour was not enough. They rejected an offer of four-and-a-half pence but finally settled for five.

One of the first major accidents occurred during construction at East Hill, Tuckingmill. Whilst laying a section of the passing loop on the incline, a traction engine (see page 42) belonging to Hosken, Trevithick and Polkinghorn of Hayle, pulling wagons loaded with flour, was forced to the north side of the road where the wall collapsed. A steel hawser was quickly attached to the engine preventing it from toppling over onto the road below.

On a more serious note there were some fatalities. The first happened on the 29th November, 1902, when tram No. 6, a single deck, struck one of the residents of the old Barncoose Union (workhouse). His injuries were so bad that he had to have a leg amputated but died later that evening. The next fatality did not occur until 1905, when

The Camborne and Redruth Tramway

a young boy of two-and-a-half years, ran out in front of a tram and was killed instantly. The driver did an emergency stop but was unable to prevent the accident. There were other deaths over the years, plus various other types of accidents, e.g., horses being frightened and bolting, also many other minor incidents.

Throughout the years of the trams there appears to have been only one recorded account of a derailment. In 1912, a double deck going too fast as it approached points in Trelowarren Street, jumped off the rails and demolished the front wall and window of Bailey's confectionery shop. The driver was deemed liable and dismissed.

On a more light hearted approach, there were other events and occasions which merit mentioning. Firstly, the "Pasty Specials"; these were the trams that left Redruth terminus at twelve noon carrying pasties and other food items. At various points along the route they were picked up and delivered to eagerly awaiting workmen and miners. A flat rate of one (old) penny was charged for this service.

Then came the "Football Specials". Local rugby derby matches between Redruth and Camborne were always well supported and needed additional trams to cater for the different supporters travelling to whichever town the match was taking place.

Another special, a one off, was "Kitchener's Recruitment" tram, urging men to enlist in

The Camborne and Redruth Tramway

the army for the First World War. The tram was decked out with red, white and blue bunting and a section of the Devon & Cornwall Light Infantry band played. Needless to say, there were not many takers.

Finally, but not least, were the "Miners' Specials". These left each terminus every morning at five thirty with a half hourly service until eight o'clock, taking miners to the various mines along the route.

It is difficult to understand how this magnificent transport system, unique to Cornwall, came to close. No doubt pressure from the Great Western Railway and the introduction of motor buses all played their part. Profits started to drop, the wage bill became higher and maintenance costs kept increasing leaving the company with a great many problems.

The inevitable decision was taken. The system was to close for passenger service on the 29th September, 1927. The last trams saw some incredible scenes; thousands of people lined the route as if attending a funeral procession for royalty. It was a very sad occasion. Over its operational years the trams travelled well over three-and-a-half million miles and carried in excess of thirty million passengers.

Although this was the end of the passenger trams, the route remained open for the mineral trams; these carried on for another seven years.

# CAMBORNE - REDRUTH TRAMWAY
## Length 3 miles 726 yards

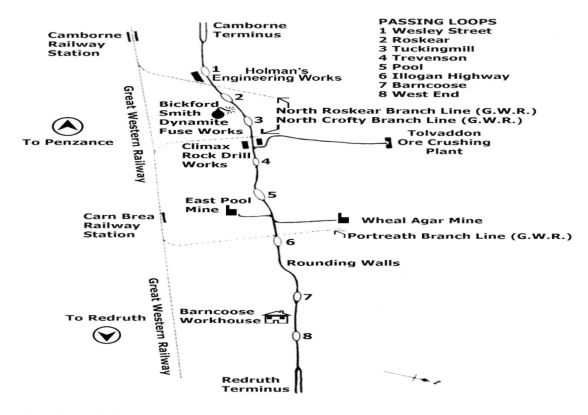

**PASSING LOOPS**
1 Wesley Street
2 Roskear
3 Tuckingmill
4 Trevenson
5 Pool
6 Illogan Highway
7 Barncoose
8 West End

This shows the layout of the tramway system with eight passing loops, three Great Western Railway mineral branch lines and the mineral tramway track.

Redruth Terminus, West End. Opening day November 7th, 1902.
Tram No. 1 at the terminus having been driven from Camborne by Mr. Hanning, chief engineer. On board were all the councillors from Camborne and Redruth, about to be taken to the depot where they were given a tour of the works, followed by tea.

Redruth Terminus, circa 1905.
The first building on the right was the old tramway office with some of the drivers in the doorway. When the tramway system closed down this building was used as the local Electricity Board shop and office.

The Camborne and Redruth Tramway                                                    13

Redruth, West End. Tram No. 7. Circa 1905
Note the lack of advertising on the tram. Carpenter's fruit and vegetable shop is on the left whilst further on is Terril and Rogers Ironfounders, makers of the old Cornish range.

The Camborne and Redruth Tramway

Redruth, West End.  "Rugby Special", Tram No. 4.
Quite often these "specials" were vastly overcrowded when local derby rugby matches took place. Safety did not seem to be high on the agenda!

The Camborne and Redruth Tramway

West End junction with Coach Lane showing the passing loop. The building on the right - Cook & Son, Cornish builder - later became Willoughby & Lenton's Garage. This site was demolished and a row of terraced houses built in its place.

West End. Tram No. 8 passing the entrance to Penventon, the home of the Carkeek family. During the Second World War it was used as a Civil Defence Headquarters, then later on the Ministry of Pensions and National Insurance took it over. In 1966 it was opened as an hotel and is still a very popular place.

Blowing House Hill. Tram No. 7 on its way into Redruth around 1907. The old Redruth County Grammar School has just been completed and is ready to open.

December 12th, 1914. The "Recruitment" tram, covered with red, white and blue bunting and a section of the D. C. L.I. band on board, going down Blowinghouse Hill. Travelling along the route they were hoping for young men to enlist in Kitchener's Army. It was not a particularly successful campaign.

The Camborne and Redruth Tramway                                                                              19

Outside Barncoose Union (now the Camborne - Redruth Community Hospital) on the passing loop, tram No. 2 on the right going into Redruth, Tram No. 3 going into Camborne. Note the absence of passengers.

The Camborne and Redruth Tramway

Tram No. 3 at Barncoose, about 1905.

Tram No. 8 approaching Rounding Walls. It is interesting to compare this and the next pictures with the road as it is today.

Tram No. 1 at Rounding Walls. Chariot Road goes off to the right, on the left is where A.T.S. (previously Taylor's) tyre services is situated.

Rounding Walls. Tram No. 7 is showing quite clearly the shape of the road. There was a story of how a local boy cycled along the top of the wall on the right. A very brave boy indeed if the story is true, as there is a twenty feet drop on the inside of the wall.

Illogan Highway junction of Chili Road looking towards Pool, about 1905. The young girls on the left look very neat and tidy with their white pinafore dresses, perhaps they are on their way to Barncoose School.

ILLOGAN HIGHWAY, Nr. REDRUTH.

An interesting picture showing Tram No. 7 crossing the G.W.R. mineral branch line at Illogan Highway. The G.W.R. line came from Carn Brea station and went down to Portreath carrying tin ore to be shipped to smelting works in Wales. On the return journey the wagons would be loaded with coal for the mine engines. The building on the right is the Railway Inn.

The Camborne and Redruth Tramway

A rather unique photograph taken outside Pool Wesley Chapel showing Tram No. 4 on its way to Redruth, followed closely by a mineral tram returning to East Pool mines having disposed of a load of tin ore at the Tolvaddon crushing plant. The Camborne & Redruth Tramway was perhaps the only system that allowed passenger and mineral trams to use the same lines.

The Camborne and Redruth Tramway

Pool, showing the workforce laying a section of the track in June 1902.

Pool. On the left of the picture is where the original Carn Brea Post Office used to be.

The Camborne and Redruth Tramway

Pool 1904.
One of the Hosken, Trevithick and Polkinghorn's steam Thornycroft engines on its way to Redruth, possibly delivering flour to Trounson's.
Tram No.2 on the loop going to Camborne.

The Camborne and Redruth Tramway

Pool, 1903.

Trams No. 7 and 8 crossing. Note that there is no advertising on the front panels, possibly because they had only recently been delivered.

The Camborne and Redruth Tramway

Pool, circa 1920, looking towards Trevenson Road with Tram No. 2 just approaching the loop. Note the interesting position of the petrol pumps; it would be difficult to stop and fill up now knowing what the traffic is like today.

Outside the Plume of Feathers, Pool, looking back to the crossroads. In the background can be seen part of East Pool, Mitchell's engine shaft headgear.

Pool. Single deck Tram No. 6 is possibly on a trial run as the driver is not in uniform. The passengers would have been given a free ride for this test run.

The tram depot and generating station at the end of Trevenson Road near the top of East Hill. The buildings from left to right are the tram repair works, generating station and boiler room.

The depot on opening day November 7th, 1902. Three trams decorated with greenery and lined up ready for inspection by the local dignitaries. Several of the drivers and conductors can be seen between the trams whilst youngsters in the foreground are hoping for a free ride.

Staff of the Camborne - Redruth Tramway, taken at the depot in 1905.

Tram No. 4 at Trevenson on the last day of service. The driver, J. Smith, moved to the Camborne - Redruth company from Plymouth because the money was better. Starting in 1903, he stayed right through to the very end, finishing the final years on the mineral trams.

The conductor, standing in the front, is S. Tellam, of Redruth. On closure he moved over to the Cornwall Motor Transport Company.

The Camborne and Redruth Tramway

The repair shop at the depot has Tram No. 1 in for maintenance and repairs to one of the bogies. Looking at the tram you can see the body resting on jacks. This enabled the workmen to lift the body up, slide the bogie out and then lower it back on the jacks.

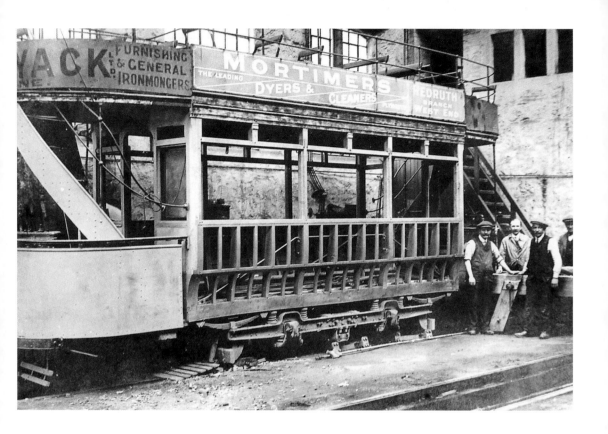

An unknown tram having quite a large amount of restoration done to the woodwork. Considering the time the vehicles spent on the road it was inevitable the dampness would seep into the structure of the tram.

The Camborne and Redruth Tramway

The Camborne - Redruth Electricity Works and Tram Depot circa 1905, with the boiler house stack on the left and the tram repair shed on the extreme right.

The Camborne and Redruth Tramway

The next three photographs show the serious accident that happened in July 1902 at East Hill, Tuckingmill.  One of Hosken, Trevithick and Polkinghorn's early engines, an Aveling and Porter, narrowly escaped falling over the side of the road at East Hill. As can be seen, there was not a great deal of room to spare, so when the engine and its load were eased over to the north side of the road, the wall started to collapse.

The Camborne and Redruth Tramway

Quick thinking prevented disaster. Using heavy timbers, the engine was propped up, then a steel hawser was attched to the large wheel and fastened to the other side of the road. This stopped the engine from moving.

The Camborne and Redruth Tramway

Using heavy lifting gear borrowed from a nearby foundry the engine was, after nearly a week, pulled back onto the road. As can be seen from the crowds in the pictures, the accident created a lot of interest.

The Camborne and Redruth Tramway

Tram No. 7 coming down East Hill. Nothing to indicate the problems incurred during the construction of the track.

Tuckingmill at the bottom of East Hill, the buildings on the left were the offices of the Bickford Smith fuse factory.

The Camborne and Redruth Tramway

Tuckingmill circa 1905.
As Tram No.3 climbs the hill towards Roskear, it passes the Bickford Smith Fuse factory.

Pendarves Street, Tuckingmill, circa 1905.
A tram on its way down from Roskear, the first shop on the right was that of Mr. Bennallack, a carpenter and undertaker.

The Camborne and Redruth Tramway

Pendarves Street, September 1911.
After numerous complaints from the council regarding damage to the road surface, agreement was made to replace and repair various sections of the line and road at the company's expense.

The Camborne and Redruth Tramway

Tram No. 8 approaching the top of Pendarves Street near the junction of Church View Road and Roskear church. This view shows very clearly the overhead pick-up wires.

The Camborne and Redruth Tramway

Trams No. 1 and 8 on the Roskear loop at the junction of Roskear Road. Note the lovely old street light on the corner.

Roskear outside the school, Tram No. 7 on its way to Camborne.

The Camborne and Redruth Tramway

Outside Roskear school, early 1920s, one of the track supervisors is watching repairs being carried out.

Wesley Street, Camborne. A tram passing the world famous Holman Engineering No. 1 Works with the well known replica of a rock drill on the balustrade. The house on the left with the bay windows used to belong to the general foreman of No. 1 Works, George Clifton. The first building on the left was the Wesley Street Post Office, later to become St. George's Printing Works.

The Camborne and Redruth Tramway

Tram No. 7 on the loop outside Centenary Chapel with Holman's No. 1 Works in the background. Note the clock above the entrance. All this block of buildings was demolished to accommodate the new Tesco. What price progress?

Trelowarren Street, Camborne, junction of Union Street, circa 1905. The building on the left of the picture was that of the Urban Electric Supply Company; it is now Norton's fish and chip shop.

The Camborne and Redruth Tramway

Trelowarren Street, circa 1905, looking towards the terminus.

Tram No. 4 in Trelowarren Street. The posting box can clearly be seen on the front of the tram; note the lovely children's pram on the right. The shop on the left with the sun blinds drawn, Mr. Bailey's confectioners, had the wall and window demolished when a tram jumped the points and careered into the building.

The Camborne terminus, at the end of Trelowarren Street, junction with Commercial Square. This shows the beautiful fountain which was presented to the town by John Holman in 1890. In recent years it has been renovated and the area around it pedestrianised.

Commercial Street junction with Fore Street, looking towards the terminus, Tram No. 1 has passengers waiting for departure to Redruth. Tom Moore's shop in the foreground was replaced by the joint London and City Banks. The "x" on the top of the building indicates where two girls lost their lives in a fire at Berriman's Drapers Shop in 1906.

Camborne terminus, circa 1903, showing the single deck Tram No. 5 ready to depart for Redruth.

The Camborne and Redruth Tramway

## Camborne Feast
### Mary Ann's Opinion of the New Street Cars  (in Cornish Dialect)
### by William Quintrell 1909

Tes Camburn Faist, says I to Jan,
Shure as my naame es Maary Ann,
I'm goin' to have a ride.
"Electric Cars" are goin' to run
The Booys and Maidens will have fun
For this es Faissen Tide.

Now put'es on thy Sunday best,
'Tes Faissen Monday weth the rest,
It's Maary Ann's Birthday.
We'll mount tha Car, we'll have a ride,
I'll take my seat close by thy side,
'Tes Tuppence all the way.

And when we git tha 'tother end,
I tell tha Jan I do intend
To look Redruth about,
For this es our Rud Letter day
To ride upon tha "New Tramway"
Our Faissen Monday out.

Thy gloves and silk hat, thee must weaar,
I want for us now to appeaar
Like "Tram Cars", "Up to Daate".

And I'll put on my silken gown
As we are goin' to Redruth Town,
Maake haaste, thee wust be laate.

Look heer's tha Car come Maary Ann,
Thee's miss her shure's my name es Jan,
'Twill lev us both behind.
Thhee'rt like the wemmen never hurry
Until ta laast, then huryy, scurry
To sarch and never find.

Hould up thy hand, "good maister stay"
We want to ride thes Faissen day
In your Electric Car.
Now Jan, git up, don't mind tha rush,
Go back you booys, why dost a' push
Like Sold-yers goin' to War.

'Tes like a palace iss plaise sure
I could ride heer, this day and more,
'Ef Jan he war so will-en.
Some contrass this to slow goin' hoss
With haaf tha truble, haaf tha coss,
I'd raather pay a shellen.

The Camborne and Redruth Tramway

I've heer'd plaise sure of Zacky Rooach,
Who used to dreve tha ould stage coaach,
I've heer'd my Unkel say,
They thoft it somethin' big my dear,
To git a ride 'bout waunce a year,
Upon a Faissen day.

That was a slow goin' thing iss sure,
They took a fortnight, sometimes more,
Raiching des-tin-a-shun.
Penzaance to Lunnon, shakin' hands
As ef 'twar goin' to Furrin lands,
And kiss'en each Re-la-shun.

Goin' all the way? Iss maister true,
I do not think that I shall rue,
Fare? Tuppence did you say?
I'll taake another one for Jan,
I'm standen' trait for my ould man,
For this es my Birthday.

'Twas Camburn Faist in '42,
I'm sixty now 'tween me and you,
I fust caame long this way.
I've been to fifty faists or more,
I've runn'd for Ribbens by the score,
And daance'd on Faissen day.

Fower-pence for two? This ride is cheap,
I'll bet you'll git a purty heap
To travel on your track.
They'll make a traade, there'll hundreds ride,
Like thee and I Jan, side by side,
From town to town and back.

Well now I spoase we must git out,
Ef we are goin' to look about,
Thee'rt lookin' Proud as Punch!
Enough to make a "Passon" smile.
I wish et war another mile,
Let's go and have some lunch!

Plaise bring us in a dish o' tay?
With cups and saucers Jan ded say,
Likewise some curran' caake,
Some bread and cream for Maary Ann,
A birthday present from her Jan,
Let's larn to give an taake.

We're in Redruth, this Faissen tide,
We've had a faist, we've had a ride,
Now shall 'es have a waalk
Up through the street, around the park?
'Tes wenter time, 'twill soon be dark,
My gracious, how thee'st talk.

The Camborne and Redruth Tramway

Lor, there she comes, she's all alight,
She twice so purty soas by night,
Aw' what a' hansom thing.
What Anti-quaated Car can stand
Beside thee, dear, thous hast command,
Jan, listen to the ring.

Good gracious, chiel, we're in the dark,
Tha' light is gone, no not a spark;
Say, hast tha got a match?
Or else soas I shall quake for feer,
But look, good lor! Tha light is heer,
Say Jan how ded-a-catch?

I ca'al this travel'n, iss plaise sure,
Good maister stop by our front door
In Tallywarren plaace.
For we've enjoyed ourselves to-day.
By ride'n on your "New Tramway",
I'm glad I sen thy faace!

Suppose ef faather shud come back,
To see the cars move on the track,
To tell the truth, he'd glaaze!
So great tha change sence faather's time,
He'd think he'd come to some new clime,
He'd surely be amaaze.

But things have moved sence mawther's dream,
We travel quickly now by steam,
On Say or Railway track.
Here for breakfast, up there for tay,
Goin' to Lunnon in a day,
'Twar out of faather's tact.

They used to take ne'er half tha night,
With tender box to git a light,
Then caame tha "Farden Candle"
But something greater meets my sight
We're in the dark, we're in the light,
By switchen just a handle.

How dost tha like thy out'en Jan?
Said the undaunted Maary Ann,
Let's have a bit a' truth.
I'm glad I've lived to see tha day,
Electric Cars along the way
From Camburn to Redruth.

We're moving with tha Coming Power,
Electric cars, fower times an hour,
Along tha new "Tramway",
From Tallywarren to West End,
Three miles and haaf tes good, you spend
Jus' "Tuppence" all the way.

The Camborne and Redruth Tramway

# Camborne - Redruth Tramway
## The Mineral Line

What of the Mineral Tramway? It opened in November, 1903, just over a year after the passenger service. Two engines, open to all the elements, were made by G.F. Milne. They were numbered 1 and 2  and both powered by two twenty-five horse power motors.

When the passenger service closed in 1927, the mineral line continued working, although it had temporarily ceased for a couple of years (1921 to 1923) due to the collapse of Mitchell's shaft. During this period of closure the company took the opportunity to enclose the cabs of the mineral engines. By looking at the early photographs of the engines, the difference can be seen quite clearly.

The mineral line section started at East Pool Mine, from Robartes shaft on the north side of the A30 and Mitchell's shaft on the south. Both branch lines converged on the main road joining the passenger line at Agar Road, going on to Pool, then Trevenson Road and on to the depot.

At the depot it wound its way through the yard, past the boiler house and exiting into Tolvaddon Road. A low embankment took the line over a bridge and onto a weighbridge where all the trucks were weighed and their loads noted. After this they carried on along a raised gantry to the crushing plant where the ore was deposited (see page 77).

Finally, after thirty years of working, the system closed in 1934.

East Pool Mine, Taylor's shaft, with the last mineral tram about to leave, in August 1934. Taylor's shaft and Mitchell's shaft, now the property of the National Trust, are open for visitors.

The Camborne and Redruth Tramway

Agar Road, Illogan Highway, outside the entrance to East Pool mine showing the mineral line branching off. Nowadays this is the site of Safeway's (Morrison's). Some might remember the old Kneebone's knitting factory and the Flamingo dance hall.

Mitchell's shaft, East Pool, circa 1903. An engine in its original form taking four wagons of ore to Tolvaddon. The young girl is a Mary Rowe and the man beside her, Johnny Pooley.

The Camborne and Redruth Tramway

East Pool, loading tin ore from the shutes, circa 1903, again with the original engine. The driver sitting on the engine is J. Williams. On the right are a couple of "balmaidens"; the gentleman in the white coat and bowler hat is Captain Toy.

Again at Mitchell's shaft with Mineral Tram No. 2 loaded with ore ready for departure to Tolvaddon. The motorman is J. Williams. When the little boy sitting on the engine grew up, he became the father of the late Tommy May, a very well known rugby referee.

Agar Road, Pool. One of the mineral trams having delivered its load of ore at Tolvaddon is on its way back to East Pool.

Taken in the mid 1920s. A mineral tram (note the engine is now enclosed) on the climb up from Pool making its way back to East Pool mine

The Camborne and Redruth Tramway

Mineral Tram No. 2, circa 1904, approaching Pool crossroads on its way to the ore crushing plant. Some young miners, with their helmets on, eager to pose for Mr. Bennetts the photographer.

The Camborne and Redruth Tramway

Trevenson loop in the mid 1920s with Mineral Trams No. 1 and 2 passing outside the entrance to Trevenson House which is now the site of Cornwall College.

The Camborne and Redruth Tramway

The end of Trevenson loop looking towards the depot. This area has been greatly altered since the photograph was taken. At one time, on the left, was Mr. A. E. Olds' garage; further on was the site of Climax Rock Drill Company.

The depot showing the mineral branch line going into the yard and passing the generating station and boiler house. The front of the old tram shed has been altered and additional pieces added to the generating station, indicating the photograph was taken in the late 1920s.

A general view of the Tolvaddon operation. In the background is the structure carrying the tram line to the crushing plant (the large building on the left). The two tall stacks on the right were the arsenic flues which were demolished when the new A30 dual carriageway was built.

Driver Smith in control of Mineral Tram No. 2, outside the old toll house at Trevenson Road. For some unknown reason, the toll house was demolished in recent years.

The Camborne and Redruth Tramway

Coming out of the rear of the Urban Electric Company's yard, Mineral Tram No. 2 is passing over the old Tolvaddon Lane. The large stack is that of the boiler room.

The Camborne and Redruth Tramway

The final day, the final tram, August 1934.

Thirty years of operation were finally closing - a very sad day. Over the years the trams made an average of eight to nine trips a day, each taking roughly one hour for the round trip. Each trip carried approximately nine tons of ore and it was estimated that one million three hundred thousand tons were taken to the crushing plant over that period of time. Driver J. Smith standing on the left with brakeman B. Sincock on the right.

The Camborne and Redruth Tramway